grown woman

VOLUME 1

poetry, short essays & Gems about
what it's really like to walk into
womanhood

BY

CRYSTAL SYMONE

GROWN WOMAN

*poetry, short essays & Gems about what it's really like
to walk into womanhood*

Copyright © 2024 by Crystal Symone

Printed in the United States of America

This book is dedicated to the girl I thought I needed to be and a testament to the woman I became.

My pain had a purpose and so does yours.

acknowledgments

Shout to God 1st and foremost for allowing me to see the purpose in the lessons I've learned. Showing up as a grown woman is a test to truly show the best version of myself.

Thank you to my friends and family for your continued support, listening ear, and love on this journey.

Finally thank you to the readers. This walk to be an author has been great. Knowing that I can make a difference or just be the reason someone may smile is the greatest gift. Stay tuned and keep the support going.

Crystal Symone

prologue

grown woman /,groʊn ˈwoŏmən// adjective

Stepping into womanhood, knowing where you've come from has no limits on where you're going. The ability to heal and grow from things meant to break you so that you can stop being "that girl "and transform into "that woman".

> " *I bloom not because I'm a flower, but because I know how to grow in any season"*
>
> -CRYSTAL SYMONE

table of contents

PART I - POETRY   1

PART II - NOTE TO SELF   41

PART III – GEMS   59

PART I

POETRY

grown woman

Grown woman

You think cause your body looks like mine you can just act any old way

Thinking one of our experiences outweighs

Like what you and I walk through are two separate doorways

But I'm leaving a doorstop in the way

Grown woman

The times have changed, but somehow this is still the same
Grown woman

Being grown is more than just doing what you please

Money isn't the only key

Independence is not the extent of what it means to be

Grown woman

What's not understood is what's below the seams
Grown Woman

Let me help you

Take my hand

I'll show you all the things I learned so I can help you understand

A grown woman is more than what's seen

There is power in your sex and strength in what you carry

But before you know all this, I'm here to help get you ready

Grown Woman Conversation Starter: What do you hope to learn about womanhood from this book?

_____

_____

_____

_____

_____

_____

_____

_____

_____

_____

_____

_____

_____

_____

_____

_____

red woman

Mood swings
Cravings
Stay far, far away
When I get like this it can only be one thing

Apart of the process of growing up
But no one told me it would hurt so bad
Cramps in my stomach
And a cranky attitude to match

Hormonal
I don't feel like being social
This is what my mom meant
When she said women feel a different type of pain
The kind that messes with my brain

It's more than just blood from my womb

I see red when I think about the controls placed on me
Living in a world where lawmakers see me
As a killer
Or someone on the pillar
Of public assistance that they hated either way

The flame that is my gender wraps its arms around me
Rights being taken away fleetingly
Not realizing I'm a part of the tree
That helps bare life

GROWN WOMAN

I'm challenged by the opposite sex
Even though they've never seen this much red
Or felt this pain that comes once a month
Instead, they are lead
By men that are unfaithful, unkind, and don't even like our kind

I see red when I think of what it means to be a woman
In this kind of state
One in which the thing that makes me different
Feels like it's a part of the bait
To make women feel inferior to men

the quiet song woman

Her mouth was like a straight line
With nothing to say
It looked like one of those cartoons
Where they didn't draw a mouth
I guess that's why you never heard her scream and shout

Her, she thought she was right
And I mean about everything
Even when she was wrong
And when this happened she just added it to her song

You see the song started like this
Her heart beating like a drum
She never really got attention, not a large sum

There was a sweet melody to what appeared before her eyes
Because she liked what she saw , she made this boy into a prize
He wasn't what she expected , once she knew him past his surface

You see she knew him from his chorus, but didn't know his structure
He was everything she wanted, but in all actuality she only saw the message
The one he wanted her to see
And because of this she was put at ease

So she let him in, like any woman would do
But suddenly his pitch changed
And even though this song started beautifully
For some reason he couldn't hear her while she silently screamed

GROWN WOMAN

For him to stop
For him to not enter
For him to not touch her there
For him to be gentle
For him to just listen to her eyes

Because they sang a song
One without a pitch
It was toneless
But if he read her eyes he would know
She didn't like this, right now she wanted to take it slow

The quiet song is what played as she lay being violated
Losing nerve to fight back
Not knowing this moment would be relived
A moment she could never forgive
Forgive herself for being so absent

Absent minded
Absent from it all

I guess that's why she has to live life stuck in the quiet song

*A poem for the women that found silence when they looked for the courage to speak.

broken-hearted woman

They say I'm avoidant ever since you last said my name
I've been real indifferent since you played my heart in your silly games
Avoidant of my plate, because how could I eat
Everything I would normally care about has taken a back seat
My eyes are red, and I can't tell anyone why
Who I used to be
Is a far cry
From what I looked like with you
It seems like all we said would happen fell through
They told me heartbreak would pass
But right now I can't envision my heart without this huge mass
It's weighing
Heavy enough to make me think
Think about the darkness
Because this weight
Is just too heavy to bare
A broken heart never killed but it feels like it could tonight
Right before the darkness swallows me
And unpredictability follows me
I wake up from this nightmare and don't let the bad feel like it can
borrow me

I suddenly remember all that you said
I suddenly remember all that you didn't do
And unlike my heart my brain can recall
All the times I said
I didn't want us to fall

GROWN WOMAN

Instead of cementing together, it was a free for all
I was free to give you all of me
And you showed your true self once you realized the true cost of being
with someone like me

Meant you couldn't do the bare minimum
Meant you couldn't just be
Meant I expected more out the deal
It takes more to impress me

You said you wanted to be my man
But entertain me if you will
A man leads and I'll follow
But you weren't really used to being allowed to lead
Even though we haven't been slaves for over 400 years you've never
been freed

I digress
I backspace from this
No time to reminisce

toxic wo(man)

I carry a torch for you
That always left me ignited
But I can't believe this flame is toxic
Because I was told
If he's mean to you
And pushes you down
What he really wants
Is to say he likes you on the playground

I carry a torch for boys like you
Who have two faces
The one that pulled me in
And the other that pushes me away

I carry a torch for words like
Narcissist
Jerk
Mean
Unkind

I carry the torch because I want to breakthrough
Visions of the real you
And not that other person you show me you can be
I fell in love with your potential
But fell out of the sky
Because I realized
I wasn't enough
And I learned to say goodbye

punching bag woman

You punched me with your words
Never raised a fist
The things you said to me
Hang in the air of our kiss
I'm sorry
Didn't mean to say
What you heard was wrong
That's just how I show my love
Show that I am strong

You punched me with your actual hands
And then proceeded to give me a kiss
Saying this hurts me more than it hurts you
Saying in your childhood it was hit or miss
Of the time's love was modeled for you
In the form of thrown fists

You punched me while entering my body
When I said no
No permission
I didn't approve of this acquisition
For you to use me
In a way, I wasn't comfortable being used
Whether there was physical contact
Or just an invasion of my space
You punched me in a tender place
One that no woman should ever face

You punched me in my freedom
With all your rules
Hit me where it hurts
I tried to listen if it meant you would keep lifting up my skirt
Knowing my every move
Because you cared so much about my safety
I had something to prove

Fits of fists
Thrown into this punching bag of a dating scene
Feeling stuck between
Compromising my rules
Or really confirming this man is a fool
Because this is the first time we've met
And somehow he can't pay for the check

My punching bag
Keeps getting hit
Sometimes I get the nerve to quit

Quit these hopes
Quit these dreams
Quit thinking about this scene

The one in my head
I saw as a teen
Where I had it all figured out
But this punching bag hangs in a cloud full of doubt

I can't take any more hits
Hits to my pride
Hits to my hope
There can be no more tropes

GROWN WOMAN

Where boy meets girl
And effs it up
I can't go through another breakup
Almost ready to put my gloves up

plan b woman

The most well-laid plans
Disappeared once she got up from laying
What was supposed to be
A session of her hips temporarily swaying
Has become anticipating

Unconventional
Unplanned
And Undesirable
These are the options

What's the value of a life
One you consider taking
Is it true this could lead to a new life worth making
Even though this decision isn't what she had in mind
Could this be a blessing in disguise
Or is this just another lie

How to save a life or take one raging
The impact of this decision, is it even worth taking
A million thoughts course through competing
Not sure which will win but these feelings are gaping
Good girls never tell I guess that's why her heart is racing
What's about to explode is her mind
A baby wasn't in the cards for this timeline

This thing between them
Was never supposed to turn into lifelong strings

Because her soul was weak
She pulled in soul ties
Most relationships of hers had a habit
Because they died

But this one
Was he even the one
One of the good guys
That took care of his kid
Or was he the one who wouldn't even buy a birthday present

Plan A was working
Exceptionally well
But Plan B is leaving her unwell
Who do you run to when every option is its own personal hell

When you keep hearing things like
My body my choice
The sentences coming from your inner voice
Conflicting with what you feel is right
If you get this choice wrong will your soul ever feel right

The most well-laid plans
Disappeared once she got up from laying
Once the sex was gone
Something within her body said this seed is staying

preyed on woman

My body grew before I did
What a shame
Men's eyes have no shades
To stop their lingering eyes from dancing
On a body that was barely of age

There would have been some signs that hinted at my lack of maturity
But when you're being led by what you see
All the other clues of true identity become skewed
The truth of the matter is
Even with honesty, you would probably still look my way
Analyze the size of my waist
You say my girlish charm is what attracted you

But with age, comes wisdom
I've had plenty of lessons
Like how as a result of being with you
I didn't have the same expectations of women your age

You didn't have to have it all together to catch me
My age somehow made me carefree
And you could easily hide your lack of stability
Like somehow your lack of mobility would go unnoticed by me

Age aint nothing but a number
Except
You used it as a basis for every relationship you've kept
All the expectations and commitments have now been swept

Under your selection for what you desire
Knowing damn well a marriage isn't what you aspire
The only thing you could teach me was how to stroke this fire

These embers and remnants of what our bodies can do
And even though you're mature the basis of your conversations is
Can I come through?

Come through and wreak havoc
Get you addicted to me
Attach my spirit to yours and decree
That I'll make you love me
Just enough to temporarily forget
I preyed over you like a gazelle
The lion in me
Became awakened
What I've done there's no mistaken

I preyed on you, and now your body and mind is mine for the taking

trauma woman

Young enough to know no one's perfect
But old enough to see that this is wrong
I know that how you treat me is a direct result of what you've seen
But does that really mean you can take the insecurities and unfinished
dreams
Out on me
There are things I want to tell you but fear that you can't handle
I know that I'm your child but I'm still my own person
The things I want are important too

Safe space is more than just a phrase when I know dysfunction follows
you
You tell me not to question you because you're an adult
So why do I get the feeling you're just as confused as me
Please don't take it as disrespect it's just that you raised me to be
curious about the world
And that includes you too

I see the way our family is and sometimes it scares me that normalcy
doesn't exist
The patterns of our lives seem to be copied and pasted into every aspect
of our life
Just because it happened to you at my age doesn't mean that I will have
the same fate

I know this isn't healthy but I want it to work because you are my blood
The dysfunction started long before you and I
But does it really have to continue in order to know it must end

honest woman

Baby be honest about where you've been
I know what you did
And what you're doing
Because I did it before
You aren't the first and won't be the last
In the realm of growing up and becoming a teen
All I ask is that you be honest with me
The sooner you understand the more free you'll be
This journey you're taking may feel like it's a lonely one
With all the changing faces, places, and hormones rushing through you
it's a lot
The world you live in is so different from my own
You live in a world where being a kid is oversexualized, exploited, and
just damn right insane

But, baby be honest

When the world and your friends instruct you not to tell me
Please do
The harshest reality of today is that you are unprotected
Even with me by your side
I know I can't protect you from it all
But maybe I can protect you from some of it
The parts I lived
And the parts you'll see

GROWN WOMAN

Baby, I know you're all grown up

Becoming a woman

Becoming you

Baby always talk to me

Always let me know the truth

No matter how hard it is

I'd rather know than watch you die from holding it in

confident woman

Looking in the mirror knowing this face of mine is made just the way
it's supposed to be
With every pimple, blemish, and imperfection
I am who I'm supposed to be

Confidence started with someone calling me pretty or beautiful
But it's grown into much more
I am who I'm supposed to be

I don't need anyone to tell me
I just know for myself
That this face was one meant for the world to see
Even if it's just little old me
I am who I'm supposed to be

I reach within myself and don't listen to the haters
I'm beautiful
I wasn't just made but created
I am who I'm supposed to be

I know of beauty because it lives within me
Not deep in the confines of the shadows
Not below the surface because he called me pretty
And not worn on my face
I am who I'm supposed to be

My weight
Doesn't dictate
Who I believe I am

My hair won't negate
The fact that I'm in charge of my fate

I am who I'm supposed to be

treasure woman

What I carry has value
It's not discounted
Bargain priced
Or undersold
I've got a jewel buried within me
That can only be defined as my sex
I can't bend a knee
To any man who wants a key
To the door within me

I wasn't always like this
You see
At one time
I couldn't close off the idea
That it was just sex
Like people passing through paying their respects

I encountered the types that acted like a friend
Only until they got
What was between my legs
But once that was over the nice guy act came to an end
He got what he wanted
And I got what I thought was deserving
For a woman like me

Sex was the one thing
Where I could agree
It made things easier but complicated us two

Because my mind became blurred with visions of you
Not being exactly what I needed but what I wanted
In the time it took you to pursue

I didn't ask for protection
I didn't ask for your hand
Or to be your girl
What I accepted was well below the treasure I carry now
And that's why you aren't allowed back into this sacred house

dream state woman

I thought I knew myself better than anyone else in the world
But when I look at what I've been doing lately
I have to ask who is that girl?

I'm not focused on the goals
I say I'm too busy

But really I'm bored

Scrolling endlessly
Being distracted is where my mind stays mentally
Numb to the fact
Maybe all I am good at
Is getting better at staying off track

Time is fading, and I can't seem to face
The fact that all I said would do has been put to the back
I'm left standing in place
Stuck on the things I said I would do

Don't ask me questions like
Why didn't I finish this
And what happened to your dreams
When the truth is I could just scream

Let out my frustration because life
Has been challenging me lately
With pop quizzes
Surprise tests

And lessons

It's no wonder why I'm always stressing
Putting my dreams in my pocket
And carrying them like a piece of lent
Visions of me taking off like a rocket

But all I can ask myself lately
Is who is this girl
Staring back at me
The one who gave up on her dreams

born & raised woman

This is for the girls that never left home
Never moved away out of fear of being alone
Born and raised
Looking at the same streets and avenues
You know where you're going
Even if people new to your town don't have a clue

You had big time dreams
Even though you were a small-town girl
Telling yourself next year
Would be the year
Your time
Finally, it would be your time to shine

To leave this city
And everything it took from you
A rose stuck in the concrete that never grew

You were supposed to be living a grand life
One like those girls on tv
Be about your business and have the key

To a world of happiness
Success
Not defeat

But all you got
Were familiar choices, spaces, and faces
All of your fear

27

GROWN WOMAN

Replaces what you really need
A new start
A place where you can be free

Somewhere where no one knows your name
But looking in the mirror all you can proclaim
You said you were leaving years ago
But somehow you're still in the place
The will to leave and start anew has disappeared, without a trace

pinky swear woman

We used to link pinkies

You used to know everything
You were my friend
It's like we were part of laces on the same shoestring

We used to link pinkies

And laugh, smile, cry
I could always count on you to get by
Between the secrets and the times we spent
But the link between us has been bent

It's strained like the way our faces would be
Once we realized we struggled to agree

We used to think the same
Hang around the same
Be the same

Identical like twins

But since last year
When leaves fell
And snow came
Christmas passed
And you never asked

Exactly when things started changing
For the worse

GROWN WOMAN

I deleted your number and now when I see you all I can get is a blank
verse
Because we used to be knitted together
But then we unraveled
Friends of friends
Associates
Anything but close

Until you were just a distant memory
All the things we shared are just a part of my brain's sensory

fast woman

You say I'm acting fast
But I'm moving slow

You say I'm acting fast
Because my shape is forming
I can't hide it under my clothes

You say I'm acting fast
Determined to stop this growth

You say I'm acting fast
Because I smiled at him
And he smiled at me
I would've kept a straight face
If I knew you were zeroed in on me

You say I'm acting fast
As if
Bad Reputation
Silenced conversations
People eye me like I'm an experimentation

You say I'm acting fast
Like you never did
Respectfully
As if I'm handling my body neglectfully

You say I'm acting fast
And showing my insecurities

GROWN WOMAN

Could you tell me that with certainty

Last time I checked
I was a woman
I think Maya Angelou established that

You say I'm acting fast
But I just can't hide this appreciation for my body
So what if you think I'm acting gaudy

You see it took time for me
I couldn't always appreciate what God sees
Or more what he created
Within me

I was looking for comfort in my own skin
And what I found was
A checkered flag at the end

The end of my second-guessing
Compressing
My body in clothes too big

You say I'm acting fast
But really
I fell back in love with myself

set the table woman

I set the table for what's to come

It's true that the foundation you're bringing is important

But it's also equally absorbent

That I saturate myself with success

I'm in my soft girl era but I still know I present the best

The best version of me with or without a man

I set the table for myself but I'm not afraid to fold the legs

And grab a chair

Making a new place setting at a table that's shared

I will ask for what I deserve and need

But don't confuse that with the fact that I'm still a boss

I set the table for what we could be, an empire can't be built by a single entity

What you bring with you is a seed

A seed I can nurture and build up into something more

More than arguments about you paying half

And me giving you wife privileges without the ring

This is a conversation about what we both can bring

GROWN WOMAN

I'm not just talking about offspring

I mean a table that can be set for generations to come

Something special for our sons, son

I want to transform this card table my parents played spades on

And convert it to the biggest table made of strength and resilience

So I say this in closing

The real question I'm posing

Is not what you can bring

But what you can add

Because it's going to take two

To build a table that can last

capital woman

Our access to money was once nonexistent
Culture, men, and government prohibited
Lack of capital had our sex
Sticking it out for our version of a white picket fence
Lowercase treatment
With capital-like offenses

Maybe Grandma couldn't do what I did
Because she was folding clothes
And singing nursery rhymes
Her balance sheet was equal sometimes
Her reliance on Grandpa to make the right decisions
But his spending habits just continued the division
Of a marriage with one person making decisions

But as for me and you we have access to a different set of blueprints
One that name drops
401k's, High Yield Savings Accounts, and Stocks
Things like credit in our own name
And jobs that pay more figures than some men can obtain

Options, we got options these days
Real Estate, Bonds, Entrepreneurship
Setting up a way to win
So we never have to go back to staying in unhealthy relationships again

shine woman

I used to dim my light
Because I thought what I was doing was right
Bypassing my own jewels
To allow someone else the chance to shine
I made myself a paragraph when really I was a headline

I dulled my shine for men and boys
Because I thought it helped them
See me clearer

Not see me as a threat
Thought it gave me less
Less of a net to fall and be in the zone
One in which friend was written in stone

I used to get rid of my shine
Because I hated attention
People's eyes on me
Equaled tension
Grinding in my stomach
It caused pain
Saying no to questions
Not thinking for myself and leading a life of suggestion

I used to avoid shining
As if showing all of myself meant reclining
Into a sofa of feelings that I would rather be
Just a piece of dull

#2 pencil
With no sharpness or sparkle

I used to dim my light
To let others shine

stand on it woman

I said it
I did it
And I meant it

I stand on it
By it
Within it
And own it

I did what they told you
Even if it was a lie

I take accountability
Because lies don't benefit me
I stood tall when I was with them
So why would my character change
All of a sudden
There's dirt thrown on my name

But it's ok
Tell people what serves you
And fits your needs
I'll be the villain in your story
So I can be the hero in mine

I build boundaries and somehow those that remained seemed to
dwindle
Things became simple

GROWN WOMAN

As a grown woman
I can't sacrifice who I am
To conform to what people want me to be

I said it
I did it
And meant it

I'm not taking anything back
Because I said what I said
And I mean that for a fact

Stand on it
Stand on these words
Stand on these actions because they are superb
Stand on what's shown instead of what is spoken

Maybe then you can understand why I've become so outspoken

I stand on top of my words
Because I am a woman of my word
I stand on top of the actions
Because they dictate how I operate
I stand on being apologetic when I'm wrong
But I also believe in standing strong
On my opinions, and my thoughts

I stand on it because no one will trample me

PART II

NOTE
TO
SELF

Please be advised these essays will NOT:

WILL NOT follow grammatical sentence structure

WILL NOT be that long-ish

WILL NOT make you cry, but may make you smile

But it will be

WILL BE mostly based on people I may or may not know

WILL BE real, authentic, and honest

WILL BE my own opinion and not that of anyone else therefore you may or may not enjoy what I write

WILL BE things that I had to live and grow through

WILL BE what I've learned not what I've mastered, because I'm not perfect

And lastly

YOU WILL BE INSPIRED AND HOPEFULLY FIND SOME GOOD STUFF THAT YOU CAN CARRY WITH YOU AS YOU CONTINUE GROWING

NOTE TO SELF

Friendship in your 20's

One of life's significant elements is friendships, and as a woman, the friends you surround yourself with can either jumpstart your growth or keep you stuck in old habits. Our desire to want to connect with other women starts at birth. The relationship or lack of we have with our mothers is the first chance we must build a connection with another woman. The ability to build long-lasting friendships isn't easy and even harder to maintain through life's changes, but in the end, it's worth it. Or so I've heard.

In my early twenties, I was easygoing with almost everyone who entered my life. Fueled by people-pleasing tendencies, I effortlessly connected with various personalities. Disliking someone or not considering them a friend was a rarity. But because I struggled with showing my genuine self a lot of these friendships died out. The ability to connect with other women wasn't always something I knew I struggled with. I embraced plans with a carefree attitude, deeming myself a "good friend" based on always showing up, pouring into others, and too much accountability. But the truth is my friends didn't always need those things that was just what I felt comfortable giving out.

Firstly, I consistently "showed up" for friends, attending events, parties, birthday celebrations, or nights out for drinks. I remember driving over three hours to visit a friend who wouldn't even call me to see how I was doing. After driving a total of six hours just to see them for thirty minutes. I "showed up" but didn't quite understand why it didn't feel appreciated. In the past I didn't hesitate to go above and beyond, offering resources and knowledge to help others. While this was my way of expressing care, many of these so-called "friends" failed to reciprocate when I needed them. When my birthday arrived, these friends were unavailable, often canceling the last minute. My envisioned experiences of having a wine down Sunday like Issa and Molly didn't align with the reality of my friendships.

Secondly, friendship manifested in my life through excessive "pouring into others," sometimes at unhealthy levels. I remember wanting to pour into my friend after she had a bad breakup. I was a listening ear offered solutions and consoled my friend at a time when I needed to do for myself. The "bad breakup" somehow turned into them making up. Somehow, I had neglected my own needs for a situation that wasn't even mine to be worried about in the first place.

Having a personality inclined towards acts of service as a love language can be both a blessing and a curse. While the desire to be seen as helpful and valuable propels you to do for others, the truth is that you must prioritize "pouring into yourself" before extending that care to others. If you can readily drop everything for a friend, you should afford yourself the same consideration.

The third aspect of my approach to friendship demanded "accountability" for how I showed up for my friends. I questioned whether I was the type of friend worthy of reciprocation. My need to be accountable for everything, even someone else's actions somehow always equated to feeling guilty. I felt guilty when I didn't hold myself accountable for my actions or inaction in friendships, and then would believe because of this I somehow controlled another person's feelings and emotions. I had to learn to be accountable for myself and not feel guilty for what someone else was doing as a result.

I'll admit, I didn't always pass this test of self-accountability. There were instances where I took too many steps back from the friendship because I was uncomfortable but didn't voice how I felt. There were also times when someone was using me, but I failed to be real with myself about their intentions and instead of ending the friendship I allowed it to continue. During my early twenties, I also did things like prioritize a potential romantic interest over my friends. I think we've all been there when you canceled at the last minute with friends because of an "appointment". Now as a grown woman and wife, I understand that my man does come first but putting in effort and time for friends is still a priority.

Taking accountability for how you navigate the world extends to your friendships. But we all need to know that accountability isn't a one-way street. Your friends are accountable for how they treat you just as much as your actions are portrayed in how you treat them.

As you walk into your womanhood, understand that friendships can endure for a lifetime or merely a season, and that's okay. Nothing on Earth remains unmoving, and this applies to your circle of friends.

NOTE TO SELF: If you're grappling with finding a new tribe, parting ways with toxic friends, or simply seeking individuals who aspire for more, be open-minded. Recognize your strength in being able to walk alone until the right time comes for you to build a supportive group around you.

NOTE TO SELF

People Pleasing vs YOU

Let's talk about people pleasing this big old elephant in every room interpretive I mean of a woman's life. More specifically, in my life. To some extent, we all want to be accepted by the people around us. A huge part of being a woman relies on being nurturing, accepting, and reliant. But a lot of times these characteristics show up in the form of people pleasing and putting ourselves second. Before we go deeper into the connection between people-pleasing, and being a grown woman, let's talk about what people-pleasing looks like in your life.

In my life people pleasing means putting others first before myself, so that I don't say no to them, which in turn means, I don't disappoint them. People pleasing, also shows up in my life in the form of avoiding conflict and trying to avoid being morphed into an "angry black woman". For some women, this is not an issue, and they could care less about pleasing someone for the sake of their feelings. Ladies, know this note to self is probably not for you, but keep reading anyway.

To tackle people pleasing you must tackle the inner you first. For women people pleasing feels like it's built into our DNA from birth because we are used to showing care to others naturally. But what I've learned as a recovering people pleaser is that you must feel comfortable not being liked all the time. Instead of thinking situations will escalate to an extinction event of your relationship we have to learn that it's okay to disagree and still love the person afterwards.

Some of the practices that have helped me become better at not pleasing others are thinking before I respond and even saying I'll answer the question later. What I'm doing is giving myself time to think before I simply "agree". Another helpful practice is to not take the path of least resistance, what I mean by that is I always considered myself someone that went with the flow of things. This isn't a bad trait but when you look up and see yourself somewhere you don't want to be more than a few times you must learn resistance. Resistance to simply agree and assert what it is you want to do.

People pleasing is a huge part of why we as women find ourselves compromising who we are for the people around us. In some respects, we believe if we can't operate in perfect harmony with those, we care about it somehow equals disappointment. But the truth is it's even more disappointing to show up for everyone else and not yourself. Lean into being you and allow what's to follow to truly guide you in the relationships you seek through others.

NOTE TO SELF

Don't Look Back

When you're walking into being the truest version of yourself you will make mistakes. Some of them can be fixed with "I'm sorry". But there will be times/ situations/ people that just have to be left in the past. Some things just must end messy and the closure in goodbye must be enough for you. Not looking back has everything to do with you moving forward in your life with no regrets. If you make a mistake, try to right it, but once you've tried your best without compromising your boundaries you must learn to move on.

I have found this to be easier said than done. Why?

Because I don't do messy cliffhangers, drama, or being ingenuine... unless I'm reading it in a book. But the truth is life won't be perfect if anything is imperfect. I had to realize it's not my sole responsibility to correct these issues as it relates to my relationships. As a woman, it's not our job to give so much of ourselves but not see the same actions returned. Learning how to take a step back and truly understand what problems were mine to pour my energy into helped me understand where I stood with people in my life. Once you stop looking back at what everyone else needs you can start being present with your own needs.

As we grow, we often see that the people we hang around have a direct effect on some of our behavior. Our parents used to warn us that birds of a feather flock together and even though it's a simple saying it holds truth. The people you surround yourself with can show your character and influence your own decisions. I remember being close in high school with Boy X. When I met Boy X, he was academically gifted, an athlete, and had a job. These were things I found attractive about him. Eventually, Boy X started hanging around Boy Z. Boy Z was not a bad person, but he just didn't have the same focus and determination as Boy X. I hung out with them remembering smoking weed and enjoying it. But at one point weed stopped being enough for Boy Z. After my then guy friend hung around Boy Z enough, he stopped having ambition. It wasn't that he didn't fit this perfect profile anymore that made me leave, it was that he cared about nothing but chasing the next high. A short while before I officially stopped hanging with Boy X his other friend had found something stronger than weed, he had moved to doing coke. I knew then that no matter how much I liked boy X I wasn't about to be involved with anyone that did hard drugs. I saw too much; I knew too much about the impact hard drugs could have on your life. Within the span of less than six months, Boy X barely came to school, lost his athletic scholarship, and his job, and had become a frequent user of coke. It hurt me to see a person I cared about begin to care so little about their life. I had seen his body, and even his mind change like day and night. But I thank God I got the message from him to step back from this person's life. He started living a life that I couldn't quite see for myself and even though I wanted to see him prosper I knew it couldn't be done with me by his side.

Once you have overcome something "don't look back" Continue building the life you need to be the best version of yourself. The new version of yourself is not worth losing just to fall back into old habits or people.

NOTE TO SELF

On My Mental

Mental health is one of the most important aspects of taking care of yourself. As I've grown up to step into my full womanhood, I've started to see my life in sections regarding mental health.

In the beginning, you make habits around what's modeled to you by your family and environment. Some of us want to blame our parents for our poor decisions, lifestyle, and mental intelligence. There is a little truth to that, but the other side of this truth is that they couldn't show you something they never knew for themselves. This applies to mental health, especially within certain communities' access to mental help hasn't always been easy to have.

But as you grow older you start to unlearn habits that are unhealthy and not good for you. It's important during this journey that you show yourself some grace. For so long mental health has gone unspoken, swept under the carpet, and just plain old muted in showing up in our lives. Your mental health isn't a once-a-month type of thing it's an everyday aspect of making sure your needs are met.

What mental health looks like in my life right now is therapy. Through this, I've learned so much about myself and my habits. I'm not going to lie, it's hard and your emotions may feel like a roller coaster. But the great thing about my relationship with therapy is that it's an open door. Once I heal or learn from what's bothering me, I can move on to living my life. My therapist always reminds me that therapy shouldn't be something you stay in forever but it's a place you can always visit when you need to.

Through therapy, you can learn more about your behavior and get help from a professional who can provide an unbiased opinion on situations in your life. The great part about conversation is it opens your mind to learning about the patterns and behaviors you've carried through your life and how they show up in current relationships.

But it's not just about what's happening in the present, therapy is also a good resource to reckon with your past. Because we are continuously growing our response to situations will change. The person you are as a girl and who you are as a woman are separate things. But when you haven't worked past the "little girl" inside she will show up in your adult life. Working past trauma, decisions, or lack of action are just some of the ways you can tackle your past.

In a time where everyone shows their best on screen and not the struggle, mental health is more important than ever. The days of being grateful for what you have can be washed away with a post of someone living a life you wish was yours. We all know how draining it can be to want to be happy but feel like it's impossible because we live a life of comparison.

On my mental ladies please take care of yourself and heal what is within.

NOTE TO SELF

The Strong Friend

Let's be honest, being a strong friend is a thankless task and a hard role to fill. It's crazy how as a woman my need to help others extends to almost every relationship in my life. Being a strong friend looks like investing in others' problems, except your own. The strong friend is the therapist, coordinator, and communication organizer. In general, the person that holds a group or relationship together.

But being "the glue" that holds things together is tiring.

And I for one, believe it's time we as women step into a new role, one that is healthier and rewarding. Moving past the mentality of doing everything yourself and instead being okay with things being solved without your initiative. It's not your responsibility to fulfill all these roles to hold up a relationship. Once you start owning your time and figuring out what's important to you, so many pieces of your life line up.

As someone who has recently been struggling to understand how friendship has changed in my life leading into my late twenties, it has been so hard not to fall back into being a strong friend. Transitioning from being invested in meeting up, showing up to every event, and answering every call is not easy. In part, it feels like it can equate to not caring enough anymore. But the truth is figuring out how you will show up in relationships that you've been in for years doesn't equal all the right steps overnight. It takes time for your friends to realize they can't have the same expectations they once held about you. Some people will adjust to this new version of you and others will see it as a negative that they can't use you anymore.

In the end, your relationship with others is based on your effort and that of the other people in the relationship. Sometimes effort is needed from you, while other situations require you to take a step back. Let your friend be a friend to you. If they care about you, they won't take it personally that you've taken time for yourself.

Being a "strong friend" is nice because people can depend on you. But when you need that mutual support in your time of need you can become resentful when you don't receive the same. To avoid that feeling start being honest about what way you decide to show up. Know that it's okay to change how you show up in relationships in your life. That is the point of life anyway to evoke change.

NOTE TO SELF

Parents

Your relationship with your parents shapes your life so strongly because we are a result of what we have seen. As human beings, we learn our behavior through modeling. The term modeling is a psychological term describing that people learn through watching others. The people we watch are normally our parents or whoever takes care of us.

My relationship with my parents hasn't always been easy and although they made mistakes, they were still an important factor in who I am today. If you're like me, your parents have probably made plenty of mistakes but because you love them you learned to forgive.

One of the biggest lessons I've learned walking into my womanhood is that I can only carry what's mine. The things my parents carried with them emotionally are just that, theirs. It is not your responsibility to live out the fantasy your parents had for their own lives. It is not your responsibility to overcome their mistakes through your actions. And it is not your responsibility to take their experiences and directly make them yours. It is not your responsibility to allow their fears to be projected onto you. When we think about illness in our family, diseases, and even habits they are often seen as things that are passed down from generation to generation. In the black community this is especially true, but has it ever occurred that we could be passing along things because our lifestyles, habits, and behaviors aren't changing? That's where choice comes in, you can choose to live your life differently even if it's not what you saw growing up.

Another thing about our relationships with our parents is adjusting our expectations. For those of us who may have parents who are a little bit harder to love because of their own bad decisions and toxic habits, it's challenging to set realistic expectations for them. As someone who once stopped talking to their mother for almost two years at one time, I can relate to adjusting my expectations. I had to take a break from a relationship with the woman that brought me into the world because my expectations of what I wanted and what she could give were not matching up. Interactions with my mom used to leave me feeling sad, frustrated, and disappointed. She wasn't being the woman I wanted her to be by making bad decisions one after the other. Once she realized she didn't have that same access to me and my siblings something clicked for her that she needed to change. I am so thankful she did because I love having her in my life. Our relationship is still far from perfect, but it is manageable. I understand now that seeing my mother as an adult who makes mistakes too has changed the way I understand her own choices. But that's not always the case, sometimes the relationship cannot be mended either because it's a danger to you or emotionally depleting. And in those cases, it's best to give yourself space.

In the end, you can't pick your parents and even though most people's intention is not to mess up their kids' lives, unfortunately, it is the result of us all being imperfect. It just so happens some people screw their kids up more than others. But in the end, because we are grown women, we take accountability that just because we didn't have the best examples, we have the power to create our version of healthy behavior.

NOTE TO SELF

Welcome to The Soft Girl Era

Being soft has everything to do with how you show up and display your femininity. This note to self is a reminder that being a woman is meant to be hard but not so much that you can't appreciate the softness you can bring to the world.

A grown woman is more than makeup, good hair, and a nice body. We are so much more because we were designed that way. A woman is complex, unique, and beautiful. We are naturally built to show our soft, vulnerable, motherly selves to the world. But being in your "soft girl era" doesn't just happen by chance, it takes a lot of work.

There are a bunch of reasons why this era of womanhood was slow to show up in my life. The first experience that comes to mind is childhood. As a child, I celebrated wearing pink dressing up, and doing all the things a little girl likes to do. But as I grew into a young woman somewhere along the line, I traded in my feminine side for tomboy habits. Things like wearing jeans over a skirt, or not caring that the nail polish on my nails was chipped were things I just didn't care about. Although these traits are a part of me they were not helpful in my learning how to have a soft girl era.

The second reason why I didn't quite hit the soft girl era was because the environment I was in required the survival mentality to show up. In your soft girl era, your focus can't be stuck in a scarcity mindset. Why, because being soft requires you to sit in confidence and security of yourself. When I had to focus on surviving it felt like there was no room to be vulnerable to others. I was wearing tools for battle not for walking in femininity.

Being a "soft girl" requires certain conditions that must be met, one of them being security.

The last reason I struggled with walking into my soft girl era was because change is hard for me and every other human being not just us women. Being able to change something about yourself takes time and patience. Me walking into this era of my womanhood to accept that I am creative, beautiful, talented, and that girl has required many failures and lessons. There have been so many times when I questioned myself about being vulnerable, open, and receptive so that people could know the real me. The changes started with me doing small things like dressing up at least one day a week. Letting my guard down with my partner and trusting him instead of always wanting to take the lead. I had to re-teach myself how to love myself and show up in the world.

Being a "soft girl" requires some inner work to figure out why you had to show up as a more hardened version of yourself in the first place. Other steps to being a "soft girl" include having a strong man who's not afraid to lead. Now this is one I struggle with myself because I am naturally bossy (don't tell my husband I said that). But baby steps are helpful to eventually allow more and more trust to be placed in your partner's hands. It's key to remember they may not do things exactly like you would. Being a "soft girl" doesn't mean you let a man trample over your feelings but it's about allowing yourself to be submissive to the natural masculine need a man has. My last step for walking in the "soft girl" era is to give grace to yourself being a woman has never been easy but now more than ever we must stand up and be our authentic selves no matter who it pisses off!

Being in your soft girl era is about you setting the standard for your life and finally taking the exhale we as women need.

PART III

GEMS

(QUOTES AND AFFIRMATIONS TO REAFFIRM THE WOMAN IN YOU)

"*Be true to yourself.*"

-ANONYMOUS

"*Save your money for the good things in life… travel as much as you can.*"

-ANONYMOUS

"*Never be scared to speak up and mean what you say as a young or old woman.*"

-ANONYMOUS

"*Embrace being you, the Lord has need of you.*"

-DENETRIA

"*You can do anything, and I mean anything.*"

-ANONYMOUS

"*It's okay to be you the world is waiting for your greatness.*"

-JANINE

"*You can't heal from what you hide.*"

-IVY

"*Nothing Stays the same no matter how bad it is.*"

-LYDIA

"*You don't need a man to have a successful journey.*"

-ANONYMOUS

" *We can't protect what we don't know you are going through, all in all we are here for your upliftment and protection.*"

-BRO NUBI AKA FATHER OF MANY DAUGHTERS

" *No matter what you are going through breathe! Know that everything can be worked through. Big or Small Just make a choice and remember that NOT choosing is a choice too.*"

-NAWARTAT MAJESTIC REIGN

" *Saying NO and not changing your choice to benefit the one you love or is in love with you.*"

-PRINCESS

" *Pour into yourself first, then fill others with the overflow.*"

-BRITNEY

" *Believe in yourself, have faith in your abilities! Without a humble but reasonable confidence in your own powers, you cannot be successful or happy.*"

-TOYA

" *No matter how old you get, there will always be a "little girl" inside of you. Love her. Nurture her. Be gentle with her. Doing so leads to greater self- awareness, self-acceptance, and self-love.*"

-SHEENA

" *Focus on self-love first and the rest will fall in place.*"

-ANONYMOUS

" *It's ok to make the mistake; just learn and grow from them.* "

-ANONYMOUS

" *Always put yourself first and love yourself. How can you expect others to love you if you can't love yourself?* "

-ANONYMOUS

" The key to good mental health = Prayer, prayer, prayer."

-ANONYMOUS

" Celebrate you by enjoying the simple things in life."

-LANITRA JACKSON

" *It's important to remember that people outgrow folks all the time. If you're not growing, you're standing still in time.* "

-JAYLA

" *Know who and whose you are.* "

-ZHATEYAH YISREAL

" *Remember to always seek God first in all that you do, and it will all fall in place.* "

-PROVERBS 3:6

" *You are enough.* "

-ANONYMOUS

" *Do not allow any man or woman to define you according to past mistakes. Always remember that you are wonderful in the sight of God, and he loves you right where you are.*"

-EPHESIANS 2:10

" *Boundaries are good things; they help instruct people on how to love and treat you.*"

-ANONYMOUS

" *Move your body it's good for your mind & soul.*"

-ANONYMOUS

" *Take breaks, and step away from the outside world, self-love is the best love.*"

-ANONYMOUS

" *Please know there is nothing you cannot do!*"

-ANONYMOUS

" *Trust your heart so you can understand your feelings, trust your mind it can provide a solution to life's problems, and trust your spirit to discern what you can't see, have faith that all things will work for your good!*"

-CRYSTAL SYMONE

THE END

OTHER TITLES

POETRY
COLLECTIONS

Speak Up

What I Meant to Say

Available at authorcrystalsymone.com

www.ingramcontent.com/pod-product-compliance
Lightning Source LLC
Chambersburg PA
CBHW070449130626

46553CB00006B/2322

9798989937905